STAMP COLLECTING

UNHINGED

STAMP COLLECTING

UNHINGED

THIRTY YEARS TO SAVE THE HOBBY

TIM CLEGG

Matador
9 Priory Business Park,
Wistow Road, Kibworth Beauchamp,
Leicestershire. LE8 0RX
Tel: (+44) 116 279 2299
Fax: (+44) 116 279 2277
Email: books@troubador.co.uk
Web: www.troubador.co.uk/matador

ISBN 9781 780881 881

British Library Cataloguing in Publication Data.
A catalogue record for this book is available from the British Library.

Typeset in 12pt Aldine401 BT Roman by Troubador Publishing Ltd, Leicester, UK

Matador is an imprint of Troubador Publishing Ltd

Printed and bound in the UK by TJ International, Padstow, Cornwall

For dad.

Illustrations by the wonderful Basia! Many thanks!

Introduction

This is not a conventional guide to the world of stamp collecting. You won't find any colour pictures of rare items, beautiful designs, or even that most iconic of stamps, the Penny Black.

For one thing, the Penny Black is a registered trademark, so we'd need permission to print it. And for another, we're assuming you know what it looks like.

Although, as an experiment, why not try and draw one from memory in the box below. Not only does that save us from possible trademark infringement, but provides for a bit of fun, challenging ourselves on the things we think we know. And don't worry if it turns out badly. It really couldn't be any worse than the attempts we made earlier.

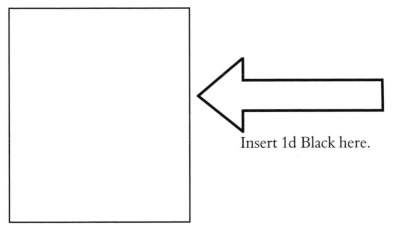

Insert 1d Black here.

Neither in this book will you find detailed chapters on how best to store your stamps, or how best to display them, or on how to use a watermark detector. The only thing we have to say about watermark detectors is that we no longer stock them, due to the number of complaints they used to generate.

Regarding stamp storage, it's hard to beat a decent stock book. And as for advice on displaying your stamps, well, why bother? Nobody's interested anyway.

Just kidding of course, but let's be under no illusion. Great challenges to the hobby lie ahead, which must be over-come if it is to survive beyond the mid part of the twenty first century.

Stamp Collecting Unhinged will touch on a range of philatelic topics, some of which are of pressing concern. It may at times seem unorthodox in its approach, but we care about this hobby, and don't want to see it slide into obscurity in the near future. Brought to you by one of the few stamp shops left in the British Isles, we'll also pass on some tips of the trade, which will hopefully lend a little more transparency to the philatelic jungle.

On the subject of greater transparency, and if condition is your thing, beware hinge remains stuck to the back of stamps. What are they hiding?

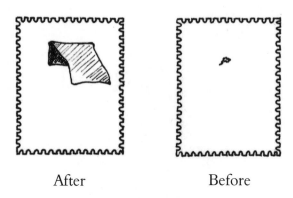

After   Before

Our shop is based in Torbay, a popular seaside resort in the South West of England, made up of three towns, and known locally as the English Riviera. There's a marina here with some posh boats and plenty of friendly visitors. The weather is perhaps a little less appealing than that of Cannes, but at least a mojito won't set you back twenty quid.

And Torbay isn't only unusual in having a marina, a stamp shop, and a fairly mild climate. It also boasts numerous Palm Trees which line the seafront and promenade, giving the resort a somewhat unique and continental feel. That these Palms are actually examples of *cordyline australis*, also known as the New Zealand Cabbage Plant, is of little concern. They look great, and Spiro would be proud.

Real   Fake

We opened the shop in 2005 and were told it was a crazy idea. We were warned repeatedly that town centres were dying, that retail is moving online, and that stamp shops in particular were closing down, not opening up. But being unhinged, we went ahead with the project regardless. Sometimes you have to take a risk to feel alive. And it seems to have been a risk worth taking.

Today we receive many visitors, both collectors and dealers alike, who naturally want to discuss stamps. It's clear that people enjoy the social aspect of visiting a traditional stamp shop, and many philatelic conversations take place. This social dimension is something hard to replicate when buying online, and is the one big advantage high street shops hold over the internet.

And this continuous stamp-shop-chit-chat led to a curious thing. With popular topics of conversation regularly repeating themselves, the script for a book effectively began to write itself, and *Stamp Collecting Unhinged* was born.

We've included the questions and subjects which arise the most, and offer our opinions with which you're welcome to disagree. It is of course a hobby of differing views. Only last week we received complaint that we'd used a postage label on a parcel. We were advised that as a result, not only would our business die, but so would the hobby itself.

This seemed a bit harsh. Postage labels are inevitable, and we are at least keeping a traditional stamp shop open. But even so, we don't believe these labels are to blame for any decline in the number of people collecting stamps today. Indeed you could argue they are actually a good thing, serving to make the postage stamp itself more exotic, and by extension, more desirable.

That the hobby has problems is however clearly unarguable. We publish this book in an attempt to help re-hinge it.

ONE

Do People Still Collect Stamps?

This is a question posed with regularity. Visitors frequently comment on the shortage of stamp shops around these days, and many are surprised to discover us trading at all. It's clear that times have changed.

Growing up as a child back in the 1970's, I recall there were at least four stamp shops in Torbay. Today, there is just the one, and whilst the explosion in online retail has naturally hit the high street, the decline in stamp shop numbers began long before internet shopping took hold.

And it's not just shops that have disappeared. The days of busy stamp clubs at every school, where children would meet at lunchtimes to swop and trade, have long since passed. Such clubs are now a rarity, and attitudes towards philately and stamp collectors are markedly different to how they once were. I remember announcing with pride at school that I'd upgraded my Ventura album to a spring-backed Simplex in shiny green. Today, I doubt children would be so vocal about their interest in stamp collecting, such is the stigma now attached to the hobby. It just isn't cool and it just isn't done. Indeed, it's now considered by many as a bit of a joke.

TWO

Having a laugh!

It's no laughing matter, of course. And please don't think it's only kids who are amused by the idea of collecting stamps.

We recently cancelled a contract with a well known phone directory, after the sales agent laughed at our request to be classified under "Stamp Dealers". A short chuckle we probably wouldn't have noticed. Even moderate amusement we could have overlooked. But this guy lost it totally, such was the degree of hilarity with which he viewed the hobby.

The incident was almost Pythonesque in its unreality, and serves as a shocking but revealing insight into how philately is viewed by many today.

THREE

The Philatelic Bio-hazard

Older readers will no doubt be familiar with the term "Stamp Bug". Once caught it was near impossible to shake off, and we used to see children wearing badges advertising their membership.

I can report with regret that the term today will more likely imply some kind of illness. Teaching English in schools at the turn of the millennium allowed me to ask students what they thought a "Stamp Bug" was.

No context was provided, and the two most popular answers that came back were insect and virus. A lad called Adam even suggested, apparently in all seriousness, that it might be a nervous disorder which caused the knee to unintentionally jerk, resulting in a random and unpredictable stamping of the foot. Or in more severe cases, feet. But very few ever suggested that the Stamp Bug might be an interest in stamp collecting.

The Stamp Bug

FOUR

Does the hobby have a future?

Some people in the stamp trade tell us the hobby has about thirty years left at best. "After that", remarked one experienced dealer, "stamp collecting will be about as popular as bear baiting", a particularly gruesome hobby, fashionable apparently in the time of the Tudors.

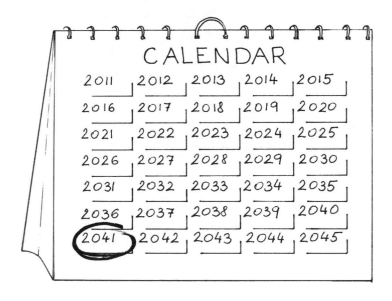

Thirty years to save the hobby might seem a radical view, but it's by no means an isolated one. It's based in part on the belief that adults only collect stamps if they already did so as a child. We don't necessarily accept this, but the argument follows that unless children of today are actively collecting, extinction is assured.

Warning: Extinction TimeLine

Circa 10000 BC – Mammoth

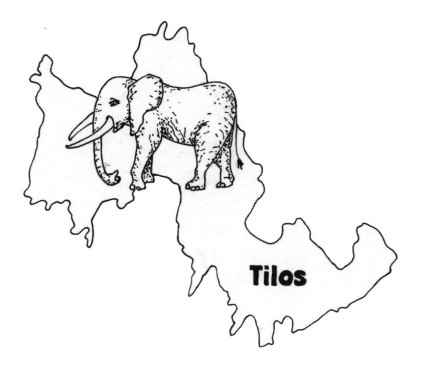

Circa 4000 BC – Tilos Dwarf Elephant

1662 – Mauritius Dodo

1876 – Falkland Island Fox

2041 – The Philatelist?

The problem is that on the whole, kids aren't interested, and this youthful indifference is perfectly understandable. If I were growing up in 2012, an age where technological advance pervades youth culture at every level, I seriously doubt I would ditch my x-box and smart phone for a stamp album. The youth of today is a different animal from generations past, and the world in which they live is virtually unrecognisable to the world of ten years ago, let alone thirty or forty.

And here's the rub. Children now live in an age where media communication is virtual and electronic, and where interaction is no longer conducted by letter. It is a slipping and sliding confusion of social networking, with forums, twitters, tweets, and blogs. It is digital and immersive. It is immediate and pervasive.

The writing of letters or postcards, and by association the concept of the postage stamp, is both obscure and redundant to today's teenager. So the sooner we stop obsessing about establishing a new generation of active young stamp collectors, the better. It isn't going to happen.

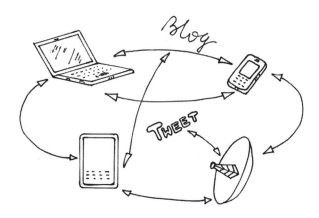

FIVE

Scape Goating

So too, the situation has little to do with that popular scapegoat, the trading card. Trading cards are actually part of the solution, not the problem, and we despair when dealers criticise this type of collectable. And of course, these cards are sadly destined to become as increasingly marginalised as stamps.

In fact, all forms of printed matter are an endangered species. Traditionally printed books will give way to e-books, just as photo albums have already given way to memory cards, and newspapers, comics and magazines will give way to websites and digital media. Printed matter is in terminal decline.

But in spite of this, children will continue to collect. As a species, we are biologically underpinned to do so. It is simply the nature of the thing collected that is rapidly changing. Today's youth collect things relevant to a virtual and digital age, such as Face Book friends, smart phones apps, You Tube videos, and rare and mysterious artefacts which await discovery in online computer gaming worlds.

I talk to teenagers who have large collections of enchanted gem stones, magical wands and cloaks of invisibility. But they are curious digital things, made up of pixels and computer code, existing only in cyber space and the imaginations of the child.

People of all ages buy, sell and swop these virtual items online, in much the same way as we used to do with stamps at clubs and meetings. So too, they often display their collections to others, but not in a Gay Ventura stamp album, or even a Simplex Medium in shiny green. They are displayed on the balconies of their online houses, in their online worlds, to their online friends.

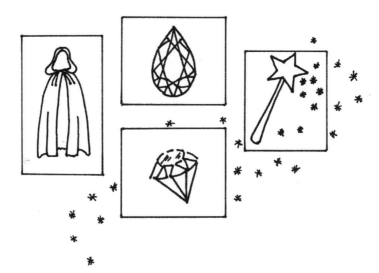

It's a lot more fun and relevant for today's teenager, than sorting through obscure and redundant bits of paper with plastic tweezers. It's a hard pill for us philatelists of older generations to swallow, but being hard doesn't make it any less true.

SIX

Little Horrors!

Every so often, parents and grandparents visit our shop with their children, keen to get them collecting. It's an educational hobby after all, teaching us much about history, geography, art and design, and we ourselves have won more than one pub quiz thanks to knowledge gained from stamps.

Unfortunately however, kids don't see it this way, and we can often guess the purpose of their visit before anybody speaks. It is betrayed by the look of horror on the children's faces.

They usually play along of course, but they rarely return. Sadly, and despite the best intentions of the parents, the glossy new stamp album will likely end up a mat for their computer mouse, facilitating the hunt for Dragon Lords and associated treasure.

And sometimes they choose not to play along at all. Last year an unsuspecting parent was purchasing a starter pack for his ten year old son, when the child suddenly turned, gestured, and remarked to all present with dead pan delivery…

"You've got to be ****ing joking"

The transaction wasn't concluded, and as we all stood in a shocked silence, the boy took out his mobile phone and started texting a friend.

SEVEN

What can we do?

We needn't necessarily despair. The idea that adults only collect stamps if they previously did so as children is perhaps flawed. We recently sold a Windsor album to a chap in his late forties, who is currently adding penny red plates. He didn't collect as a child, but was given a World Cup first day cover around the age of twelve. The gift was motivated by an interest in football rather than philately, and yet this singular and almost accidental incident proved enough to bring him to the hobby in later years.

And this is not some isolated anecdotal account. Many of the new adult collectors we get, and who are surely representative of the situation, are first timers. And from chatting with them about how they got started with stamps, the common thread seems to be a childhood familiarity with something thematic. This suggests that whilst we clearly need to introduce kids to stamps in some way, we don't need to ensure they are actively collecting. Which considering they're not interested, is quite handy.

EIGHT

School Person Collections?

It is somewhat remarkable that the term *School Boy* collection remains in common usage today. To imply that only boys and not girls collected stamps as children is certainly dated at best. Yet *School Person* sounds awfully clumsy, so perhaps we could talk of *childhood* collections.

And however we choose to call them, it's often suggested that we pass down these collections to our kids, as a way of introducing them to the hobby.

Whilst the sentiment is again commendable, when we consider the state of the albums which are brought into our shop, we worry it's as likely to put people *off* collecting as it is to start them. Old, tatty, smelly, and often Philatelic Bio-Hazards in a very real and literal sense.

Indeed, introducing the children of today to stamps needs to be carefully thought through. It needs to be relevant, contemporary, and acceptable within the context of the peer group.

NINE

Hand Held

Trading cards are always acceptable to youth culture because children and teenagers are the primary target audience. And yet, trading cards are remarkably similar to stamps.

They can be mounted in albums and checked off against catalogues and lists. They can be traded at school with other collectors and friends. They can be admired for their detailed artwork and design. They can signify stories, historical events and cultural interests. And, they can sit neatly alongside other collectables as part of a wider collecting interest.

Perhaps most importantly however, they can be held in the hand. They are real. They are certainly not meaningless as some would unwisely claim, and when philatelists criticise these cards, they should bear in mind that they criticise a product which encourages children to collect things which are real as opposed to virtual.

So if the handing down of your childhood stamp collection isn't quite having the effect you'd hoped for, why not buy your child a few packs of trading cards, and include some sets of stamps and perhaps a First Day Cover. Such items fit with ease into a collection based around football or Harry Potter for example. With a little luck in the future, they will remember their Harry Potter trading cards, and their Harry Potter presentation pack, and the beautiful set of stamps that wait inside.

It's important to broaden the introduction of stamps through this themed approach, which must include non-philatelic items, because the true battle ahead is to encourage children to engage with real objects, with hand held objects (other than, of course, their smart phone).

As already said, trading cards are actually part of the solution, along with signed photos, models, medals, commemorative coins, anything in fact which is relevant to the wider collecting interest of the child, and is both real and acceptable to the peer group.

Kids don't need to become active stamp collectors yet. The great discovery of philately can come later in life, when people begin searching for things with greater meaning. When Face Book friends have become transparent and are clearly not the friends we thought they were. When playing online games has become less than thrilling, and when we turn our attention to the reassuring authenticity provided by objects which can be held in the hand.

I'd rather buy a child a packet of football trading cards, a signed cover by George Best, and a 1966 World Cup presentation pack, than a stamp album and a packet of hinges that are going to remain unhinged.

TEN

Improving Perceptions

Of course, there are other problems to address, none more so than the image of philately today. There's no denying that many people see stamp collecting as just plain dull.

In our view, and we suspect in yours too, nothing could be further from the truth, but we can't simply expect potential new collectors to take our word for it.

As with anything in life, we can always seek to improve perceptions by updating, rethinking and re-inventing. Consider Shakespeare by way of analogy.

Teaching Shakespeare has become a real challenge in the twenty first century, as any teacher will confirm. It's regularly seen as outdated and old fashioned. Many children recoil at the mere mention of the name before they've even opened a book or seen a performance:

**"Old-fashioned and boring. I don't understand it.
What's the point?"**

Not dissimilar to the views held by many on stamp collecting, so it seems a good analogy to use. And as disinterested as students might be, Shakespeare is part of the National Curriculum, and statute decrees it must be taught.

So let's take Hamlet. If Shakespeare is at the top of our literary canon, then Hamlet is probably at the top of Shakespeare. It carries serious cultural weight. But how to sell it to today's youth?

ELEVEN

Who put the E in Hamlet?

The beauty of Shakespeare comes from the wealth of interpretation for which it allows. The text and language offer multiple meanings which transcend the norm and rightly elevate the work to iconic literary status.

Hamlet is set in Denmark, and was written around 1600. The students are yawning already of course, but all is not lost. To start with, it's quite literally a bloody good play. And if we suggest an interpretation that is both contemporary and unusual, then things change.

Post-structural analysis allows for the play to be read as a powerful warning against the use of drugs. The young Prince Hamlet is not only fighting against his murderous step-father, but also battles addiction to dangerous hallucinogens. Framed in this way, and the kids are suddenly listening, engaging with a text they had previously considered pointless or irrelevant.

Of course, such a radical interpretation will meet with resistance from some traditional Shakespearian scholars. However, if this re-invention engages students who would otherwise show little interest, then in our opinion it can only be good thing. And of course, meaning is constructed by the reader, not given by the text, and this reading of Shakespeare is perfectly legitimate.

Likewise, aspects of philately can be updated and reinvented. Unless we are able to establish contemporary relevance, the view that stamp collecting is old-fashioned, boring and pointless will remain firmly in place. When considering how to do it, we could do worse than look to the world of medal collecting.

"Why look you there!

My father, in his habit as he lived!"

TWELVE

The story behind super fish Al

A medal dealer once told me that in his view stamp collecting was superficial. He argued that there often seemed to be little sense of narrative or clearly defined purpose, and the whole process seemed somewhat random or one dimensional.

I didn't fully understand his points at the time, so he explained further that with medal collecting, the medal itself is actually somewhat insignificant. It's the person *behind* the medal, their biography and their story which is of real interest. Medals that come with supporting documentation such as letters and photographs are therefore much more desirable than medals without.

This thinking to some extent challenges traditional methods of stamp collecting. It demands a context which is so often absent in philately, particularly at entry level to the hobby. As such, randomly allocating stamps to country pages could seem a little pointless, as might gap filling, or hunting down catalogue identification numbers in the quest to complete a particular country.

Interesting

Very Interesting

Indeed, what should be clear over the last one hundred and seventy years is the transient nature of stamp collections. They are often put together with great care and effort, only to be passed on and immediately broken down. The fragments of the broken down collections are then recycled, forming new collections for new collectors. And of course, this cycle continues. It is the wheel of life of the stamp collection. To take a step back for a moment, and consider this from a detached perspective, is to recognise the futility of the process as perceived by many potential new collectors.

However, by shifting the focus away from the stamp itself, as beautiful a work of art as it may be, and towards the potential stories which surround it, new paradigms and collecting methods can evolve.

Indeed, if the process of forming and building our stamp collection tells a story as we proceed, it is certainly not a futile activity. It is more like reading a book, only with much greater opportunity for interaction, and much greater freedom of direction.

We need to prioritize this notion of narrative.

Consider how Stanley Donen used stamps in the classic Audrey Hepburn movie, Charade. It doesn't come much better than that. And whether we derive the narrative from the image depicted on the stamp, or simply the contents of the letter to which the stamp is affixed, it really doesn't matter, just so long as it inspires interest and encourages us to continue the journey.

Even as with Donen and Hepburn, a fictional utilisation of the stamp is welcome.

THIRTEEN

 *Think*

We need to be creative, to think outside the box, and we need to promote new and exciting ways of organising collections. The traditional method of collecting by country according to catalogue number is absolutely fine. I do it myself and I enjoy it. But certainly it is too limited in scope to ensure the survival of this great hobby. We need to appeal to a post modern youth (pun firmly intended) who won't be tied by rules and linear concepts. And whilst we firmly believe therefore that the future is best served by thematic approaches, we also need to carefully consider which topics are currently trending.

FOURTEEN

Stamp Vamp

Birds and Trains are great thematic subjects of course, but in this age of Twilight, we wager the SG Guide to *Vampires and the Undead* is going to appeal more to the collectors of tomorrow. And although the Royal Mail do issue commemoratives which facilitate such contemporary interests, the scope surrounding this thematic title is *far* greater than might appear at first sight. Or even bite.

Yet we often fail to prioritize new ideas and fresh thinking when it arises. A recent magazine article, inspired by photos of David Cameron posing with the new Downing Street stamp, suggested a thematic approach based on personal connections and life history. It was an inspirational article with great potential. It was also single column in size and black and white. I wish it had been given the same full colour spread afforded in the same magazine to the more traditional thematic of Post Boxes. In fact, I'd have put it on the front cover. It's exactly the kind of creative thinking we so desperately need.

FIFTEEN

Is the cat a con?

It's a common complaint, that all too obvious disconnect between stamp catalogue values and the reality. And it's a damaging complaint too.

It's a question often asked by non-collectors who may have inherited a collection they wish to sell. So too, beginners trying to understand what catalogue prices mean are often confused by the seeming inconsistency surrounding the subject.

And because there's no quick and easy answer, the impression can be given that philately is a mysterious and rather peculiar hobby, lacking in transparency and clear pricing structure. Indeed, there is a view that the stamp trade deliberately *encourages* a sense of mystery around the subject, in order to retain some kind of "control".

Whilst we don't believe it's quite that extreme, there is something that regularly differentiates how stamp catalogues are used when compared to the price guides belonging to other hobbies.

Take coin collecting as an example. Dealers selling coins rarely seem to quote catalogue values at all. In contrast, many stamp dealers will quote them at every available opportunity. And this neatly identifies the problem:

Stamp catalogue values are used as a selling tool

A comparison between adverts selling stamps and those selling other collectables such as postcards, autographs, coins or medals should confirm this observation. Stamp ads often seem to originate from a culture concerned more with cat value than the item itself, particularly regarding entry level material. A recent online listing offered the following:

1883 6d Green, used.
Cat £200. Buy it Now... only £10

The photo of the stamp showed it to be a weak green, yet the note found in the stamp catalogue that washed out colour renders this issue virtually worthless wasn't mentioned. The figure of £200 was quoted to encourage a sale, rather than to provide a helpful or realistic market valuation of the stamp. So too, it will quite likely be sold to an entry level collector.

A more extreme example of course, but it's interesting to note that where the differential between the cat and selling price is quite small, such as with GB Queen Elizabeth stamps, we find catalogue values are suddenly not quoted at all.

This selective use of cat value undermines the hobby. When the above 6d Green is brought to us for valuation or part exchange, beginners are understandably confused when advised the figure of £200 is pretty much meaningless. It has been used by the seller as a selling tool, and is not any reflection of the stamp's actual market value.

SIXTEEN

A Black Art

We have witnessed people likening stamp collecting to "some kind of black art", precisely because of this confusion. It isn't necessarily the catalogues themselves which are the problem. They serve as points of reference which can provide a useful indication of relative scarcity if nothing else.

But when certain types of collections regularly trade at around 10% of their catalogue value, eyebrows are understandably raised.

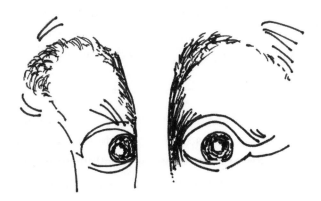

We live in an age where people crave for greater transparency and clarity in all things, from MP's expense accounts to the storage and content of our medical records. The confusion and mystery surrounding cat value shouldn't be under-estimated. It remains an obstacle in both attracting and holding on to new collectors. Most worryingly in our view, it is a tangle now too late to unravel, such is the extent to which it is embedded in the philatelic culture.

So if we can't unravel it, we should at least distance ourselves from it. Catalogue values should be quoted sparingly, and with thought, serving as genuine points of reference, with detailed context provided.

If describing a collection as having a total catalogue value of £4000, we should clarify this is based on purchasing the stamps individually and in a specific state of condition and usually at the very top price. This might sound obvious, but experience suggests it isn't at all clear to those new to the hobby, and to those thinking about taking it up.

If selling a washed out GB Victorian stamp, and we *really* feel the need to include a meaningless catalogue value, then at least clarify that the figure of £200 is dependent on condition and good colour.

We don't apportion any blame here. It is how the culture has evolved, and the goal posts are currently set. And if a dealer chooses to stop using cat value as a selling tool, he or she could disadvantage themselves in the short term, in what is still currently at least a fiercely competitive market.

However, it's a problem and it needs to be addressed at some point. To distance ourselves from catalogue value is surely the right thing to do.

SEVENTEEN

What's your favourite stamp?

For some reason, this question is asked more than any other, and at the risk of sounding a little unoriginal, we confess there is little escape from the lure of the Penny Black. We don't care that it isn't, contrary to popular belief, particularly rare or valuable. It's just iconic and it's damn fine.

So too, visitors who don't collect stamps repeatedly enquire about it, and on discovering its affordability, often purchase one as a souvenir, such is its status.

It's also a stamp around which you can build a whole collection. For the more traditionally inclined collector, there are of course different plate numbers and cancellations, and a whole host of varieties. But the Penny Black also lends itself perfectly to the idea we've been discussing of exploring stories and narrative. This was a stamp often attached *directly* to the letter sheet, without an envelope being used. So if the letter survived, then so did the stamp, along with the contents of the manuscript. Now, consider all the letters and documents from the mid-nineteenth century with stories to tell, which are underpinned by the iconic status of this most desirable of stamps.

Certainly, when wondering how to introduce philately to children, this is a stamp kids are going to cherish, and it doesn't cost the earth. And if it comes attached to the original letter sheet, the child is also introduced to the personal story behind its use, along with the reason for its existence. It isn't simply an abstract *stand alone*. Indeed, it's so much more than just a stamp, and every home should have one.

Top Tip. Remember to look out for Penny Black **Plate Number 11**. This is quite rare, and easy to spot. Unique to this plate is something known as the 7 O'clock Ray Flaw. Look under magnification at the star in the top north-east corner of the stamp. This flaw shows a missing ray in the seven o'clock position, as illustrated below. It turns up on all Plate 11's with the exception of letter positions GE and GF.

EIGHTEEN

Over Value Under Value

If the Penny Black is often considered rarer than it actually is, there's another stamp we like for quite the opposite reason. The British Two Shilling Brown of 1880 might not be the most famous or beautiful stamp ever produced, but it is perhaps under-estimated in terms of scarcity. An unassuming stamp that could easily be overlooked on an album page, it is in fact considerably rarer than the £5 Orange.

Shortly after its production, the post office took the decision to scrap it, and consequently many sheets were destroyed. Only 77,620 copies of the Two Shilling Brown were therefore issued. Now compare this to the £5 Orange, which boasts nearly 247,000 issued stamps. And although we do not advocate buying stamps for anything other than collecting pleasure, this Two Shilling Brown is a stamp we rate very highly.

NINETEEN

You don't advocate stamps for investment?

Generally speaking, no we don't. It's important to recognise that many stamps are destined to lose value from the outset. Consider those "Limited Edition" type collections, usually bought by monthly subscription and costing thousands of pounds to complete.

They turn up in auctions as job lots, often estimated at around £50. They are of course usually attractive and well presented, and if purchased in the knowledge that, like a new car, they will devalue the moment you take ownership, there shouldn't be a problem. This in fact applies to the majority of new issue stamps, and certainly to most stamps issued in the last forty years. It isn't investment material, and ideally it should be collected for pleasure.

However, even the "better" stamps need to be treated with caution. Back in the seventies, the 1929 PUC £1 was pushing £1800 in unmounted mint condition. Today, it sells for about a third of this. Investments go down as well as up, and our view is that stamps shouldn't be traded like stocks and shares. This is happening to Chinese stamps right now, with enormous prices being achieved for certain items. The two key words here – "right now".

Condition is also of paramount importance with investment. The slightest damage can result in disaster, and stamps are made of paper, and paper is vulnerable over time. Spilling coffee on your gold sovereigns might not prove costly. Neither might damp behind the safe where your gold is locked away. However with stamps, both handling and storage are real issues, and this is almost always overlooked when considering the merits of stamps as an investment.

So too, the indexes used to suggest significant rises in the value of stamps are based on a very small number of extremely rare items in premium condition. These indexes have little or no bearing on 99% of the stamp market.

And then there's the question of liquidity. It is sometimes said that stamps are a liquid form of investment, but we're not so sure. Stamps can't easily be sold in a matter of hours like stocks or shares. Auctions can seem to take forever before you see any money, and selling directly to dealers can take co-ordinated effort. (See Chapter Twenty Three).

However, all this being true, if you buy wisely and take care of your collection, it is of course possible that you will sell at a profit in the future. And even if you do take a loss, there will at least be some financial return, which can't be said of every hobby of course.

TWENTY

Why is the restoration of Art ok, but stamps "no way"?

It is certainly true and often commented upon that whilst art restoration seems perfectly acceptable, the repair of stamps is frowned upon to the extent that it is a taboo subject, not to be discussed. Dealers and philatelists have claimed that they risk their reputation for merely mentioning the subject. But it's no secret that stamps which feel a bit under the weather are sometimes made better at "stamp hospitals".

In the art world such restoration, along with any subsequent increase in value, isn't considered a problem, because a note of the restoration is recorded, and this forms part of the provenance of the painting. However, with stamps, no record of the repair is made at the time of restoration. There is *no provenance*.

We often rely therefore on Expert Committees identifying and recording the repair by way of certification. Not only is this a costly process, and as such uneconomically viable for less expensive stamps, but it also takes place *after* the event so to speak. Repairs are identified long after they have been made, and long after any financial gain from such activity has been procured. As such, it cannot be considered acceptable in the same way as it is within the art world.

TWENTY ONE

Rembrandt's Night Watch

The temptation to repair and restore stamps is also fuelled by the importance placed upon condition. And whilst I recognise that material market value is dependent upon condition, I must say that, personally, I quite like damaged stamps.

I like the fragility of the stamp. I like that it is made of paper, and will suffer imperfections and damage as it travels through distance and time. I am interested in these imperfections, and in how they might have occured. It is surely part of the fascination, and it is *certainly* part of the journey.

I sometimes think of Rembrandt's masterpiece, The Night Watch, which can be viewed at Amsterdam's Rijksmuseum. This huge oil painting had been darkened over time by muck and varnish to such an extent, that it was wrongly believed to have been depicted in moonlight.

As a result, it was incorrectly named the *Night* Watch. It wasn't until the 1940s that the mistake was realised, and the painting was cleaned. However, the title stuck, and quite right too. The "damage" had simply created a different effect, but one of no less value or worth.

TWENTY TWO

Seahorses for courses

It is interesting to note the wide difference of opinion held by collectors, and indeed dealers, regarding condition. To start with, it's all rather subjective, and one person's fine used is another person's good. Equally, some won't consider anything other than unmounted mint, whilst others are happy with a hinge mark, and many believe the notion of unmounted was only introduced so dealers could inflate their prices.

Likewise, there are numerous collectors who aren't put off by an ironed out crease, a perfin or a crayon line, and I even meet those who prefer off-centre stamps. As one chap joked with me recently, when does an off-centre stamp become a perf shift?

Certainly, a 1913 Seahorse which is perfectly centered will cost you more than one which is off-centre, but if I'm honest, I personally wouldn't want to pay the extra premium.

It is of course, seahorses for courses, and views on condition and by extension restoration will remain grounded in subjectivity. There is nothing wrong with collecting only the best examples available, but equally, there is nothing wrong with taking a less particular approach, even to the extent of embracing the damaged stamp. And you'll certainly pay less for your collection, without necessarily suffering financially, should you ever decide to sell. Indeed, it's easier to sell a Penny Black with three margins than it is with four. It's cheaper.

TWENTY THREE

What's the best way to sell my stamps?

There's much written on this subject, and articles on selling your stamps make regular appearances in monthly stamp magazines. Some of these contributions are in fact private adverts dressed up as articles, and the conflict of interest should be clear. And for all the words and all the advice offered, it's really very simple. The first thing to recognise is that **selling a decent stamp collection is the easy part. It's the buying that's hard.**

When we try to buy stamp collections, we are competing against everybody else who is interested in the same. However, when we are selling, those people aggressively competing to buy become our audience.

There are countless companies, auction houses and dealers fighting hard to buy your stamps. A browse through the pages of any stamp magazine will confirm this. So too, the Stamp Dealer section of our local telephone book tells a similar story. All the entries in the 2012 edition are advertising to buy, not to sell. As were all the entries in 2011.

As a seller (assuming of course it isn't a childhood collection which will typically command little value and even less interest), you will have no trouble finding a buyer. It's simply a matter of getting the best price, and balancing this consideration against the amount of effort you want to put into the sale.

Follow this Four Point Plan:

1. Send it away to one of the high profile auction houses who advertise for material. They will often have it collected by courier at their expense.

2. They will send you back an offer. We have no reason to believe it won't be a fair offer. If this offer meets your expectations, and you don't want to put any more work in, accept it. Job done.

They could of course recommend that you include your collection in one of their sales instead. But bear in mind, you will likely lose around a third in commissions of the eventual price paid, and the reserves might be quite low and as such risky. You'll also wait a long time before you see any money.

3. If you want to achieve more, and you are willing to devote extra time to the cause, ask for the material to be returned. You will have to pay the return postage costs, but these shouldn't be prohibitive.

You now have your stamp collection back, with a fair valuation. However, dealers compete hard with each other to buy from auctions, so common sense suggests dealers will beat this initial offer.

4. It is now simply a case of the more dealers you can contact, the better. And remember, you have the initial valuation which underpins all future negotiation.

You should end up with a better price, but you will also have expended more time and effort in the process. It is up to you to decide upon your priorities. It's that simple.

TWENTY FOUR

Treasure Hunting

There's no denying that a big part of stamp collecting's appeal is the treasure hunt aspect. We are often asked for tips on finding bargains or what to look out for. There's nothing wrong with this of course, as long as it doesn't exclude everything else the hobby has to offer. So here are a few random and eclectic tips which we hope will prove useful…

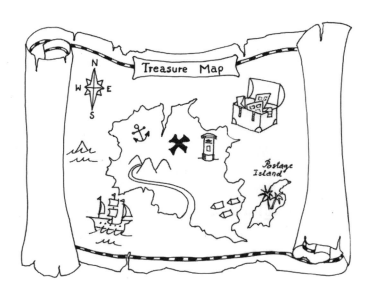

TWENTY FIVE

First Day Covers

A stamp auctioneer recently wrote that he wasn't a fan of First Day Cover collecting. He argued that cancelling stamps on their first day of issue is not a rare event, and as such, he can't see the point.

Whilst there is no obligation to like First Day Covers, this struck us as rather a peculiar argument. By the same token, the issuing of a stamp is not in itself a rare event, but I doubt he would argue there is no point in collecting stamps.

So too, the appreciation of stamps and covers shouldn't necessarily depend on rarity in the first place. Although, there are of course many instances where cancelling on the first day of issue is rare.

And some of these instances are in fact relatively recent, and you don't necessarily need deep pockets to obtain them. Consider Booklet Panes on cover.

The Royal Mail sometimes re-issues booklets with amended details such as re-arranged inscriptions, altered text or amended postal rates. These re-issues are not heavily advertised, and as a result are seldom cancelled on the first day of issue. They are highly desirable to the specialist collector, yet can turn up in fifty pence glory boxes.

Consider the 1996 £1 Booklet, issued July 8th. Not only was it re-issued on 4/2/97 with a corrected postage rate, but a further printing was made on 5/5/98 with the Overseas Postage table removed. These second and third printings are often missed, even by experienced dealers.

We recently sold the 5/5/98 booklet pane on FDC for £48. The dates don't tend to be listed in regular cover catalogues, but they can be found in GB stamp catalogues. Our advice would be to do a bit of research in this area. It could lead to some very profitable purchases.

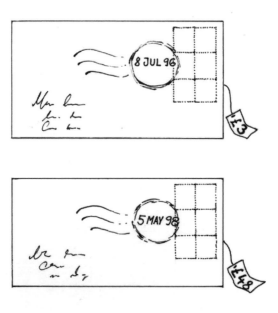

Whilst on the subject of First Day Covers, I'd like to add a personal point of view. I'm also a big fan of plain FDC's. They usually catalogue at much less than their illustrated counterparts and can sometimes be purchased for next to nothing. Yet they often carry an authenticity beyond that of the illustrated cover, and offer an affordable collecting area with scope and potential for further development. Of particular interest are those which served a genuine commercial usage as opposed to being primarily a philatelic item.

And don't be put off by hand addressed covers, or those with light damage, as long as the price reflects this of course. Many collectors do prefer a First Day Cover which shows signs of actually having been through the post.

TWENTY SIX

Mackennal Perf 14

In August 1911, the ½d Mackennal Green was issued in error with perf 14. It's easy to miss of course, but is in fact very rare, and sells for hundreds of pounds.

It turns up on postcards from the Great Yarmouth area, and the stamp is tied to the postcard by a Great Yarmouth CDS, dated around August 1911. Always check boxes of postcards from this area that fit the profile. We know somebody who found an example priced at around one pound, not once, but twice!

½d Green + (GREAT AUGUST 1911 YARMOUTH) = check perfs!

TWENTY SEVEN

Spotting the genuine Collection!

By genuine, we mean the collection is exactly what it appears to be. Perhaps old time, or substantially unchecked, it is the work of a collector put together for the purposes of collecting.

A contrived collection on the other hand is a deception. Designed for the sole purpose of selling, it has been carefully assembled to appear more valuable than it actually is. It is engineered to give the false impression of something original, exciting and intact.

And it happens all the time. Genuine and old time collections command a premium because they offer the chance of real finds, whilst contrived lots cynically pose as originating directly from the private collector or source.

Learning how to spot them not only reduces the chances of making a bad buy, but as they often turn up at auctions, can also save you a great deal of time spent viewing. If attending a stamp auction with over a hundred mixed lots, it's a real bonus if you can quickly eliminate collections which are essentially deceptions. Here are a few pointers that could help...

- Lots which include archaic accessories concern us. For instance, those early types of tweezers which look dangerous to both stamp and man.
- Add to this a packet of early type stamp hinges, a dog-eared catalogue and a dead watermark detector, and the alarms bells really start. Are they included to convince us the lot is old time?
- Envelopes and packets of loose stamps clearly marked as "*Unsorted*" or "*To check*" worry us too. Do collectors really write these words on packets of stamps?

- Be cautious of question marks, ticks and similar annotations written on the album page next to stamps. Who put them there?
- Do they seem to make sense or do they seem deliberately obscure?
- Always be sceptical of any written figure or value, in particular those found next to unusual items such as imperfs, proofs or sheetlets which are difficult to verify.
- We see misleading values all the time, often written in

foreign currencies to further obscure the issue.

- Studying the hinging in a collection can be as revealing as studying the stamps.
- Lift the stamps to enable a clear view, and compare the types of hinge used throughout the album.
- Are they all an early type, a modern type, or a mixture of the two?
- If a mix, are the modern hinges being used on eye catching or seemingly better stamps?
- If modern hinges are frequently found covering older hinge remains, it's a remaindered collection that's been refilled. Collectors, from our experience, don't tend to collect in this way.
- People often buy old and impressive looking remaindered albums, and refill them for the purposes of resale. Needless to say, some thought goes into the "refilling".
- Check mint stamps by flipping them over. Make sure they are not stuck down or adhering to the page.
- Mint Victorian looks attractive and valuable, and will catch the eye as you flick through the album. Is it however, actually re-gummed or even used with faint postmark?
- On a related note, Penny Blacks apparently unused are often washed, and need to be carefully checked. So too, if a seller lists them or indeed any stamp as "apparently unused", assume the contrary.
- Victorian embossed issues are often doctored with added backing to appear cut square. This makes a big difference of course to their value.

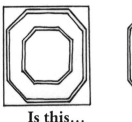 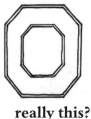

Is this...   **really this?**

- Official overprints need to be treated with real caution. If an expensive one sits in the middle of a page, and hasn't been specifically mentioned in any lot description, assume the worst. A classic description will read "Useful GB Officials with better noticed". If the seller isn't confident enough to identify the better ones, ask yourself why not?

- In fact, any stamp whose value is dependent upon an overprint needs to be treated with caution, especially if it isn't identified by a seller.

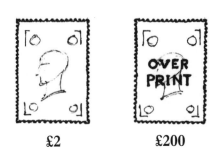

£2   £200

- There are many stamps that have an expensive looking appearance, but actually carry relatively little value. Obviously, we can't list them all here, but by way of example...

a) Reprints of expensive stamps. Beware for example

Heligoland, Indian Feudatory States, Samoa Express, Transvaal (esp. 1892 £5 Green), German and Italian States, and China.

b) Third Reich *mounted* mint, and especially the end of the period such as later Brown Ribbon issues.

c) Falkland *Dependencies* 1948 Silver Wedding. (A classic flag for the contrived lot).

d) British Commonwealth High Values which have been *fiscally* used.

e) Early Japanese Revenue stamps look great! Usually not worth much though.

f) GB Pre-decimal booklets are often of surprising little value, even up to the 10/- values.

These are just a few common examples. It takes some experience of course, but every time you are surprised that an item you thought valuable is in fact not, *make a note of it.*

Consider how it was framed, presented and included within the collection.

With experience, these observations and items will soon become "flags", and in combination, they will begin to flag up the contrived lot.

TWENTY EIGHT

Buying at Auction

The discussion of contrived lots naturally leads here, as people often seek to sell this type of collection through auction houses. Clearly, auctions provide a degree of anonymity for the vendor, and there is also the popular belief that sale rooms are a good place to buy.

And it is true that buying through public sales can prove profitable. Remember though, you'll have to outbid everybody else, and likely pay the auction significant buyers premiums. And the genuine collections rarely (but thankfully from a buying perspective, not always) go unnoticed.

So too, you need to know what you're doing. Simply turning up and expecting to secure a bargain is beyond unrealistic. And, there's the very real risk of having a total nightmare. We've all had them, and anybody who claims otherwise must be very fortunate. So once again, a few tips…

- Use Public Auctions, which allow people to attend and offer the greatest transparency.

- Familiarize yourself with the catalogue. Auction catalogues are like cryptic crossword puzzles found in broadsheet newspapers. Over time you get used to the style of particular auction houses, and begin to read *between the lines* as it were.
- For example, the term "Good Lot" might suggest it is owned by the auction house as opposed to a private vendor. Likewise and as previously mentioned, terms such as "apparently" should be treated with scepticism.
- View as many mixed lots as you can, even ones you're not intending to buy. Seek to differentiate the genuine from the contrived, and study how they have been described.
- Always check realisations against estimates, particularly on the mixed lot section. You'll no doubt start to see patterns, for example, the "Come and Buy Me" estimate.
- "Come and Buy Me" is a stock in trade estimate for auctioneers. Last year we bought a huge quantity of stock in twelve boxes that was estimated at £50. We paid over £1000 with commissions, yet the £50 estimate was no error or oversight. It was very deliberate.
- Reasons for low estimates are two-fold. They encourage people to physically attend the sale, generating visible interest and excitement (the hope being, as one auctioneer told me, that the lot goes ballistic).
- They also suggest the Auction House in question assigns conservative estimates as a general practice. **Do not ever assume that all estimates in the same auction are therefore low or conservative.**
- The best advice is to ignore estimates completely, other than for comparison against your own valuation and the actual realisations.
- These comparisons enable you to deconstruct how the

66

auction operates, and how it arrives at estimates for different types of material.

- Always remember that the estimates are never likely to be uniformly applied. For example, popular lots that will certainly attract bids are often assigned low estimates.
- **Don't go off-piste.** Stick to the lots you have viewed, and the valuations you arrived at.
- Do not be tempted to continue bidding beyond your valuation, on the assumption that if another person is still bidding, you might have undervalued it. He or she may be thinking exactly the same about you.
- And **don't ever bid out of frustration**, particularly on a lot you haven't viewed. If you are getting blown away on the lots you were after, walk away to fight another day. The biggest disasters are always purchases that have been made at auction out of frustration. Always.

TWENTY NINE

"If you could do just one other thing to help the future of the hobby...?"

We talked earlier about the huge popularity of online computer games, and we think there might be a way of harnessing this popularity in order to create thousands of active stamp collectors. Across the globe. Overnight.

It's important to recognise these are not video games in the traditional sense, where you play alone against the computer, or with a couple of friends invited around for the evening.

Known as MMORPGs (Massive Multiplayer Online Role Playing Games), millions of players log into these games to play alongside each other all over the world. They role-play characters such as knights or wizards in virtual worlds created in cyber space.

These virtual worlds have towns and cities, with shops, taverns, banks, and post offices. Postal systems are incorporated into the game mechanics, allowing the player to purchase a virtual envelope. After adding an online message, the envelope can then be posted to another player, using one of the many virtual post boxes scattered throughout the gaming world.

However, there are no stamps involved. Once posted, the envelope itself is cancelled directly by postmark to prevent re-use. In other words, it functions rather like pre-paid postal stationary.

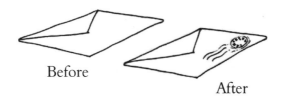

Before

After

As stated, the first M in MMORPG stands for *massive*. One gaming company alone has an estimated 12 million worldwide accounts. If the designers of these games incorporated stamps into their game-play, alongside the envelopes and post boxes that already exist, an army of stamp collectors would be created instantly.

By including limited edition stamps and perhaps the odd missing colour or two, those same people who currently dismiss the idea of stamp collecting in the real world, would be actively seeking the digital versions in the virtual world.

You can see where this might lead. The virtual stamp within the game would introduce the concept of stamp collecting to millions of children overnight, with the rarer stamps soon finding themselves displayed alongside the enchanted gem stones and cloaks of invisibility.

There are organisations with a vested interest in the future of stamp collecting who have the means and influence to explore this idea, and move the hobby forward into the twenty first century. They should start without delay in our opinion.

THIRTY

Final thought from a mild but misguided Monaco (Phil)

It just so happens as we sign this book off to the printers, that we do so on a lap top from a hotel in Monte Carlo. (We are assured the palm trees here are most authentic).

Real   Real

We came here to visit MonacoPhil 2011, a philatelic event heavily advertised in many UK stamp magazines as something "not to be missed". It seems to us however, MonacoPhil is an event that for the most part, and for most people, can *only* be missed. There is simply no other choice.

On the positive side, entrance to the Royal Philatelic Society Exhibition, held in the Top Cars Museum, was free and open to all. It clearly took a great deal of effort and commitment to put together, and formed an impressive display.

Much of it centered round an aesthetic appreciation of the stamp itself, or the history and development of stamps in a particular country. And whilst most were magnificent, the displays which really stood out for us were those held together by a broader narrative context, with two in particular.

We have talked in this book about the idea of the story behind the stamp. We have alluded to medal collecting where narrative is so important, and we have argued that the notion of narrative needs to be prioritised. We have also suggested that stamps should be considered alongside non-philatelic items and other collectables, as part of something wider in context and less linear in form.

"Extracts from a Wartime Diary" was a quite wonderful and narrative-driven display, charting historical events through a clear awareness of the story to be told.

So too, "1940-45 Denmark" used a combination of both philatelic and non philatelic items to relay a fascinating account. These two displays alone made the trip worthwhile for us.

It is therefore a real shame that one sensed such frustration and disappointment amongst so many visitors with the event as a whole. We heard the most criticism being expressed in the Salle du Canton trade hall, where the attending dealers had their stands, and visitors probably felt they could speak more freely. And the theme of this criticism centered on a perceived elitism.

For sure, a close reading of the MonacoPhil program reveals it's not just the welcome cocktail that's invitation only. "Open to all" appears just three times, while "on invitation" turns up nine times. Rightly or wrongly, the impression given is one of exclusivity, and the irony of an event "not to be missed" certainly struck home with many of the visitors to whom we spoke.

We met philatelists who had spent time and money travelling to support this meeting, and who clearly felt disappointed and somewhat excluded. Even the Monaco Stamp Museum, situated right next to the exhibition itself, apparently failed to see any wisdom in waiving the admission fee. It would have been a small but meaningful gesture.

To us, it all seemed like a step backward, elitist and out of touch, at a time when the hobby needs to be moving *forward*, if it is to survive beyond the fringes. And whilst it is of course fine to have first and second class stamps, our view holds that people shouldn't be made to feel that way about themselves.

We'd like to thank you for reading, and whether you agree with some, all or none of our opinion, we wish you the best of luck with your future philatelic pursuits.

Coming soon… *Stamp Dealing Unhinged.*

For further information please visit:
www.torbaystampcentre.co.uk

Torbay Stamp Centre
67 Belgrave Road,
Torquay
TQ2 5HZ
Tel: 01803 211001